Little Big House: Why, How, Who

By Glenn A. Ridler

Second Edition Edited By Morgan Ridler

Little Big House Gallery: Shelburne, MA

ISBN 978-0-692-83931-7

Contents

Acknowledgements/Dedication   iv

Preface to the Second Edition   vi
     Morgan Ridler

Introduction   viii
     Christine Baronas

Laying the Foundation of Little Big House   1
     Glenn A. Ridler

Life as Art, Art as Life   7
     Morgan Ridler

An Artist and Art Historian (Father/Daughter)
Discussion on Zen, Materials, and Humor   9
     Glenn A. Ridler and Morgan Ridler

Illustrations   13

Acknowledgements/Dedication

This book is dedicated to the individuals named below (and to the few forgotten over time), listed in alphabetical order:

Christine Baronas * *
Marc Bellanoit *
Becca Brown *
Bob Cantius *
Barbara Charkey *
Stan Charkey
Ellen Roy Clark
Al Dean
Bob Dolan *
Linda Driscoll
Doug Gaudet
Ed Hack *
Lynn Haven
Jeff Hillock
Paul Hofmann *
Steve Hofmann *
Charlie Hunting
Curtis Hunting
Rita Jaros
Gary Johnson
Jan Kounitz
Barbara Levy
Chase Mankowsky Moulton
Janet Mankowsky
Steve Mankowsky
Linda Morey
Dave Patrick
Ed Phelps
Rod Roberge *
Nelson Schifflet *
Larry Steinberg
Lloyd Szulborski *
Dennis Wakefield

Inspirational Teachers: Paul Harris and Brian Watkins

* These people provided extraordinary amounts of time and effort

Preface to the Second Edition

The first edition of this book, published in 2009, coincided with the exhibition, *A Chronicle: Laying The Foundation of The House, The Erection* at the Little Big House Gallery. It celebrated the contributions of the many friends and the family of Glenn Ridler, who made the construction of the Little Big House possible. Over the last eight years the gallery, located on the ground floor of the house, has organized a number of exhibitions of Ridler's work including *50 Years of Drawing, Heavy Metal* and *Tubes.* Close friends of the gallery – Deborah Baronas, Peter London, and Pacific Palumbo – have also exhibited their latest works. With the ongoing success of the Little Big House Gallery, we are thrilled to present the second edition of *Little Big House: Why, How, Who.*

Since the first edition new scholarly research has prompted Ridler to reconsider the context of the Little Big House and necessitates an update to the story of his monumental living/live-in sculpture. In retrospect, the ideas and influence of Zen can now been seen as a critical influence on Ridler's formative years and an underlying theme throughout his 50 plus year career. The enlightening book *Nothing & Everything: The Influence of Buddhism on the American Avant-Garde 1942 – 1962* by Ellen Pearlman has stimulated Ridler to reassess his links to Buddhist and Zen ideas.[1] Ridler, an ardent atheist, does not consider himself a Buddhist, however he has been inspired by Zen teachings. Ridler discusses these themes with this author in as interview included in this edition.

We have also included newly published photographs that further document the remarkable construction and development of the house and gardens. The Ridler/Baronas family and the Little Big House Gallery hopes readers will enjoy this revised edition. We have expanded distribution with the goal of increasing awareness of this important building and encourage the continued examination of the Little Big House as both an art historical monument and an evolving living/live-in sculpture.

Morgan Ridler, Ph.D.
May 2017

---

[1] Pearlman discusses the important teacher D.T. Suzuki, John Cage, Fluxus, Happenings, Abstract Expressionist, and the Beat Poets and their connections to Zen Buddhism. The ideas introduced in Pearlman's general interest and unrefined text needs further scholarly study. Ellen Pearlman, *Nothing and Everything: The Influence of Buddhism on the American Avant Garde: 1942 - 1962* (Berkeley: Evolver Editions, 2012).

Introduction

Glenn A. Ridler started physically erecting Little Big House in 1972. In 2005, he declared it complete. This exhibition is a demonstration of how it was done and, as much as can reasonably be discerned, why it was done.

In Glenn's statement he *really* starts at the beginning and gives us insight into his creative development. The influence of his family, his education, and his inclination to invent are integral to his story of laying the foundation of the house and creating a work of art in which to live.

Glenn does not limit his thinking and takes risks with ideas, and materials. In 1972 he bought $5,000 worth of pine boards and hoped the house would actually go up.
He enjoys inventing methodologies and weaving functions together and the house is his largest example of that. It demonstrates Glenn's ability to integrate creativity with function.

Ridler designed and built Little Big House while concurrently teaching thousands of art students how to develop ideas and methodologies. During his years as a teacher, he worked on Little Big House with help from his students, fellow teachers, friends and neighbors. This exhibit is intended to honor those who inspired and participated with him in building Little Big House.

Glenn's story, the reconstructed model, photographs taken during construction, and an essay by Morgan Jane Ridler, doctoral candidate in art history, are all included in this catalog. Enjoy it.

Christine R. Baronas

Laying the Foundation of Little Big House

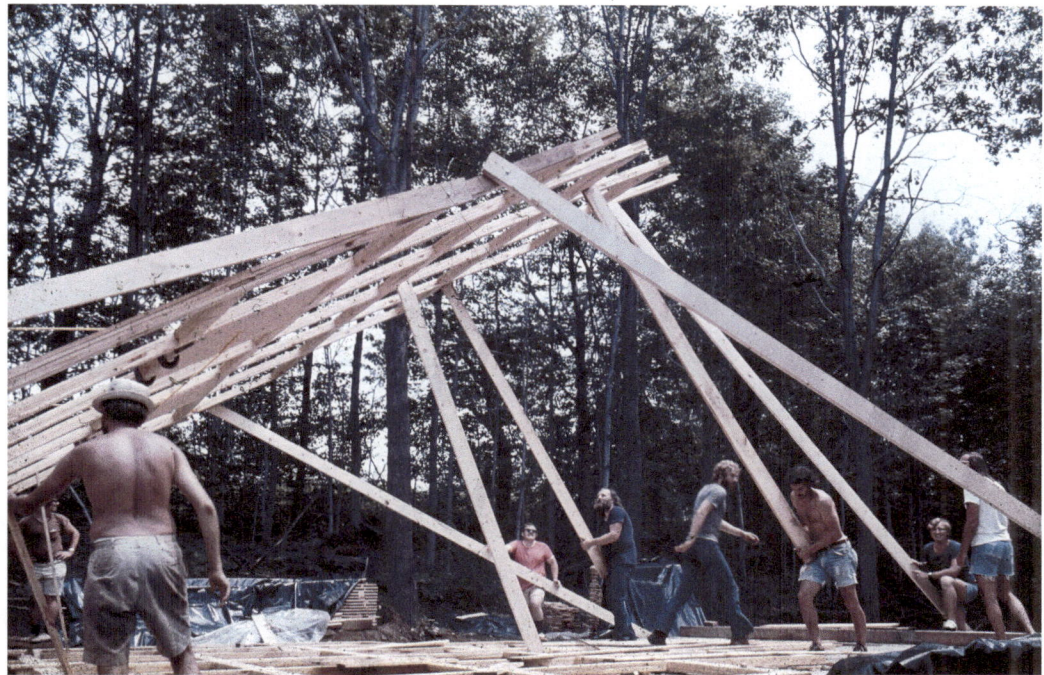

Figure 1: *Erection 1*, 1972

The foundation of Little Big House was laid firmly in psychological primal goo.

As far back as I can remember, my parents wanted to own their own home and talked about their dream house in detail. Of course there was more than one dream house - there was mother's, which remained fairly consistent, traditional, and middle class; and there were my father's dream houses, one of which was round and the other which was very small; just one good size room and brick.

As we went for rides in our 1946 Dodge all over northern New Jersey looking at houses, my parents ran a critical dialogue: too big, too small, too close to the road, "Can you believe that color?" These houses remained dream images because my father was an unskilled laborer whose best job was as a janitor in a bank. During the depression, at the age of 14, my mother was a silk mill worker. Children were employed as warpers because their hands were smaller and better adapted to run the tiny silk threads through the looms. Later she worked as a check out clerk in a supermarket. She always kept a running total of the customer's bill in her head because she did not trust the machine and if her machine was short she would be docked the amount. She was very good at arithmetic. Money was so tight that we had no telephone until I was a senior in high school in 1960.

Perhaps it was the legacy of my parents' dream, but as an adult, I became obsessed with having a house. At first, I was content to buy a house, but it soon became apparent that I needed to build my own. This need to build it myself also had family roots since the

more "handy," macho members of our family, had built their own homes. This was out of the question for my father, even if my mother and he could have afforded to build, because my mother did not consider him "handy." Believe me, mother ran the show. Yes, dad was not very good with his hands, but he was not as inept as mother thought. Her perceptions of him were warped for several reasons. First, my mother's brothers and her father were by trade builders and painters, and by temperament, insensitive clods. They delighted in putting down my father's efforts to build or repair things. Secondly, a mild form of Muscular Dystrophy handicapped Dad.

It was not until I was in college, that I began to see my father with more empathy and even to identify with him. Until then, I shared what seemed to be everyone else's dim view of my dad. The truth was, he was a kind, gentle man and he quietly passed on to me many of his funny little skills and his playfulness. He taught me to play checkers and pinochle before I went to school. I became very good at both and as a teenager I won the checker championship of Paterson, New Jersey. My interest in art began with watching him copy greeting cards with watercolors. During my junior year of high school, Dad got up at six o'clock every Saturday to drive me to special art lessons. He was insistent that I go to college and let me use the family car to drive there while he took the bus to work. We were not a well-educated family and I was the first person on either side of my family to go to college. I went on to major in art and now live my life as an artist.

So, in some way, I built my house for my parents even though they did not really like or understand it. In fact, they probably lost sleep over what they thought was my crazy move from the New York metropolitan area to western Massachusetts where there were bears, cows, and not much else. "You bought a hired hand's house and 10 acres, for the price you paid – how good could that house be?" my mother asked, not knowing that in 1968 real-estate prices were unbelievably low by city standards.

When I first started planning the house in 1970, I was unaware of the roots of my motivations. It was only after many years of thinking about it that I began to see connections. Houses started to appear in my paintings around 1967 and my graduate thesis exhibition consisted of five minimalist house and roadscape paintings, which were simple archetypal abstract houses (Figure 2).

In 1968 while I was teaching design and drawing at California Polytechnic College in San Louis Obispo, I was asked by an architect instructor to act as a prospective client for one of his classes on designing residential houses. The students asked me many questions about my needs and preferences. One of my comments was that I would enjoy a house that had a sense of humor about it. The class was silent; faces were puzzled. After a few minutes one brave student asked, "What do you mean by that? Can you give an example?" I turned to the blackboard and in a flash of insight, drew what three years later I would build and call Little Big House.

I always had an interest in architecture and while in Spain, the buildings and structures of Antonio Gaudi dazzled and inspired me. His Parc Guell showed how I might build a structure with a whimsical, if not humorous quality about it.

In the late sixties and early seventies Pop, Minimalism, Conceptual Art and Happenings were occurring one after another. I was an art student at Montclair State College in New Jersey and very influenced by these movements through the talks and writings of Allan Kaprow and John Cage. Cage maintained that art should make people mindful of their surroundings and induce them to find aesthetic pleasure in everyday life. Kaprow predicted that in the future artists would stop painting and would become preoccupied by the space and objects of everyday life, blurring the boundaries of life and art. The idea of art outside conventional spaces, and not made to sell but as a means to contemplate, enjoy and interact with, inspired me. John Dewey's *Art as Experience* in which he speaks of High Art as being a totally integrated experience also impressed me. Dewey described an art that embodies aesthetic, emotional and intellectual satisfaction – art that could sustain me.

Exposure to these ideas inspired me to make a building that was creative on many levels. First, I wanted the method of construction to be original. If I used conventional building techniques, I would get a conventional building. I had studied a local barn built in 1790. It was huge, with massive beams and a slate roof, yet it was still square and straight and truly beautiful. I wanted the look of post and beam, but lacked the knowledge, skills or tools to do the job, so I experimented with a variety of ways to fasten boards together and found that a simple stacking of boards, glued and nailed, was the strongest method. In fact, even after soaking the boards in water for several days, I could not separate them. The number two pine boards I used were very inexpensive at the time: the glue was "Titebond". As a student at Montclair State College I had a course called "Design in Materials" in which I had three different teachers, each with his own angle, yet all encouraged experimentation. I applied these experimentation techniques and explorations of materials to my creation of a unique building technique. In order to test my idea of this technique, I built a scale model using the technique. The original model was destroyed in a hurricane during the early construction.

When I first started building. My long time friend Bob Cantius and I were living in tents next to the building site. We stayed with friends the night of the storm but we left the model on site, as it was too big to take with us. The model was destroyed when we returned. I always missed having it, so recently, I rebuilt it (Figure 3).

In the full-scale house, on the cement slab, I laid out a grid 4 foot on center and stacked the 1 by 6 boards with large overlapping joints glued and nailed to each layer. There were originally four layers, which I thought would be strong enough to raise the wall in one big piece, much like a barn raising (Figures 1, 4 – 7). In the model, I used three layers and easily raised the wall with fishing line and reel, which translated into ¾-inch strong rope, a come-a-long and truck. This turned out to be my first big learning experience. Some properties of materials, like stiffness, are not proportional in scale. The walls bent. They bent a lot. In fact, I knew nothing of traditional building techniques and in looking back, I wonder how I had the nerve to start my project at all. Nevertheless, it worked, and when all four walls were raised it looked like a large modular Sol Lewitt sculpture. I was tempted to leave it like that. I realized I could put glass in all the squares. This fascinated me.

Despite this urge, I continued with my original plan, which included creating a child-like image of a house: simple, archetypal, with window boxes and eventually, checkered drapes much like a house you might find in Snow White and the Seven Dwarfs. In the process of getting a building permit, the selectman who was in charge asked me to draw what the house would look like on the back of the form, which was one sheet of paper. At that time, there was almost no building code. The selectman happened to be the man from whom I had bought the land; I made the drawing, which looked like a child had drawn it, and he said, "So you're an art teacher, eh?"

The house is not unique in its image, but one that is in everyone's childhood and subconscious mind, although, everything is oversized. The front door is about 11 ft. high. At the time, I thought I might be a surrealist and I considered the house a Jungian archetype. Now I know I am more of a conceptual artist. My idea was to have the house look like a little cottage from the road, and, as people approached it, to realize that the house is much larger than they thought and it is they who are small. I wanted to create an illusion. The optical illusion turns everyone into children, capturing the child-like quality and humor I described to the architecture class in California. The front doorknob is nine inches in diameter and hand thrown on a potter's wheel by my friend, the ceramicist Barbara Charkey. The technique of wood lamination continues inside, in the doors and even in furniture. Some original interior doors were so thick they were very heavy and in some cases were replaced. Artistic vision and practicality don't always mesh. Although the house is a sculpture, it is also a home.

A question emerged, as to how this project could be financially possible. I had a large exhibit of paintings in 1970 and had not sold any. I remember feeling the paint was worth more while it was in the tubes. I knew that I did not want to end my career with a barn full of paintings nobody wanted. I also knew I did not want to sell my house. The solution was a project that had intrinsic, as well as extrinsic value. I know that warm, dry, pleasant spaces have intrinsic worth, worth a bank values. I developed a large amount of equity, which I have tapped into several times, and sent my daughter to college.

When I first started building, I was not married, but I knew I wanted children and romantically hoped that the house would attract a woman. Some male birds build a nest and call for the same reason. In addition, I thought it would be very interesting to see what effect an art house would have on a child. I did get married. While the house did not originally attract my wife, I did marry a woman who loves art. Morgan, my daughter, is a very skilled artist presently studying for her doctoral degree in Art History. I realize that the house may not have been the cause of her interest in art and it is more likely a result of the fact that I was an artist and her art teacher that sent her in this direction.

In retrospect, the biggest problem I had was the fact that I had designed the house from the outside in, the opposite of what an architect would do. The great architect Louis Sullivan said the famous words, "Form follows function". In this case, the floor plan was developed over years. The first year found me in one small room on the first floor. For heat, I had a wood stove with chimney that was just a pipe that went out a hole in the siding. The bathtub, with a piece of plywood on top, served as my kitchen table. It was a tough winter: poor heat, no room, no siding, no second or third floors. Several factors made progress incredibly slow: first, I did not know what I was doing, and so I had to learn many skills as I went along. The frame of the house was one thing, but the electrical and plumbing are not things that allow for creativity. In addition, I kept running out of money and would have to refinance often to in order to continue. In addition, I did not plan to do everything myself but that is mostly what happened. The notable exception was the brick chimney built by Ed Hack, a friend from high school. Originally, he was going to teach me how to do it, however after watching him work, I knew the learning curve was excessively long and steep for me. We worked out a deal: he would help me on the weekends and in exchange, I would supply all the beer he could drink, all the steak he could eat. We ended up filling the negative space in the chimney with beer cans.

The first roof I put on was just rolled roofing material, but when it came time for the finished roof, I wanted split cedar shingles, so I hired an ex-student of mine, Curtis Hunting and his friend, to do the job. Curtis had a little experience doing this type of roofing and that was the extent of my professional help. That is not to say I had no help; good friends helped in many other ways. Some were colleagues from the local high school and some were ex-students. A few of us would work all week on laminating a wall and on the weekend, there was to learn later that this was much the same way locals raised their barns 100 years earlier.

The late 1960s and the early 1970s was a time of great communal awareness. I doubt today, whether I could gather 20 or so people to do this for a few beers. In the late 1980s an addition was put on the north and east sides by another friend, Nelson Schifflet who owns Valley Home Improvement

In 1968 I purchased my Shelburne, MA property from Francis Barnard. A group of people from New York City bought the rest if the large farm on our hill and I bought the hired man's house as a separate parcel. We were all college graduates with many advanced degrees between us; a couple of doctors, an anthropologist, an art history major, etc. We were young, hip, and looking for a new life style, a back to the earth movement. Some of us had done little with our hands and knew even less about farming, yet we were professionals who wanted to be organic, to be connected to the land and to each other. The locals believed we were a commune of hippies. We were not that. We were a group of free thinkers, who made many mistakes adapting to our rugged hilltop. Many of the mistakes were mine. For example, one March my dog Spot and I went to the farm to get some manure for the garden. I wanted to get manure on the snow to feed the garden as it melted and so I pulled up to a spot and started shoveling. I left the truck running and at one point, happened to look at the rear wheels to see that the truck was quickly sinking through the frozen crust. I got in and tried to move it out but rapidly it sank and the cab filled with green liquid manure. Dog Spot and I escaped by climbing out the windows. I took off all my clothes and my green Dalmatian and I ran back to the house. I called my real farmer neighbor, Vern Mitchell, to come and pull my truck out. Vern almost had a baby laughing! He could not look at me without laughing. It was embarrassing, yes, but not enough for me to call it quits.

After 34 years, the house is complete with lovely gardens that frame it beautifully, thanks to my wife Christine Baronas (Figure 10 and 11). It has in fact, become something of a local landmark and has been written about several times in local newspapers and magazines. I now have an art gallery in it to display my art and that of other local artists.

A lifetime project takes one out of the normal flow of developing an artistic career. I was too far from New York City and it took far too long to complete. In some way, my whimsical house is an albatross, draining my energy and money; I am, however, proud of it and enjoy it every day.

As for the question 'can art and life be one?', I think art comes from life and they embrace each other. I remember that Oscar Wilde said "Life imitates art far more than art imitates life"

Glenn A. Ridler

June 2009

Life as Art, Art as Life

Some artists work a lifetime perfecting and searching for how to express themselves and few are able to achieve a balance. For many artists from Leonardo to Van Gogh, there is an endless struggle to create and find the harmony between art and life. Glenn Ridler, trained as a painter, sculptor and modernist, carved out his own creative environment and has attempted to bridge the gap between art and life. Life became art for Ridler when he built Little Big House, making a reality a dream as well as synthesizing a lifetime of lessons in modernism.

Uniting painting and sculpture, architecture, conceptual and environmental art, Ridler created a monument to the freedom of the 1960s and 1970s. It is a complete reformulation of what a home looks like and what a child's vision can become. Imagine your earliest drawing of a house, your childhood doodles. It probably included a rectangular façade with a steeply pitched roof. In the middle was a large front door, flanked by two large windows, perhaps subdivided into four panes. In front of your imaginary home a front path leads to the door, flanked by flower beds. On the roof a chimney billows smoke. This is a simple home, no ornate decoration, no dormers or wings, but idealized. It is the tranquil, peaceful, happy home that we all long for.

The Little Big House started as an idea of a house. This universal and idealized conception symbolized a home and reduces all houses into one, an archetype. This simplification and essentialism is characteristic of Ridler's modernist training. Modernism, for critics like Clement Greenburg, involved each art's embrace of their qualities and mediums, no longer hiding behind illusion. Painting should be flat paint on canvas like Jackson Pollock not an illusion of space or three-dimensionality. For the modernist Mies van der Rohe, the building was a box and his skyscrapers scream: "less is more." This essentialism and simplification was one of the major elements of modernism, which Ridler absorbed at Montclair State College in New Jersey and at the California College of Arts and Crafts in the 1960s.

In addition to the formal concepts of Greenberg, Ridler also experienced Pop, Minimalism and Conceptual art. He was seduced by the color theory of Josef Albers and the poetry of the Beats. He was inspired by the shaped canvases and minimalism of Frank Stella and the happenings of Allan Kaprow. Art was part of culture and community. The cultural upheaval of the 1960s challenged the conventions of living: long hair and all. It was the zeitgeist, the sense of the times, to create art in life. Joining his modernist training with the conceptual and environmental art of the 1960s and 1970s, Ridler used all of these influences to create a complete merger of art and life.

For the Little Big House, not only is the universal conception of a house important, but scale is also important. The house at first looks small. From the road it looks like it is one room. But the eye is fooled. When approaching from the road the house seems to grow. By the time one has reached the yellow front door looming in front of them, one realizes the door is 11 feet high. In reality, the building is three stories tall. The front windows are not on ground level but are floor to ceiling on the second floor. This optical illusion is experience as well as seen. One feels small.

The scale reveals an important element of the Little Big House, humor. The fun house mirror affect of approaching a growing house insights laughter. The comic element is critical. While Mies's skyscrapers are simplified and reduced they are serious, sterile and cold. Ridler's simple house is comical and child-like. Much like Calder's *Circus* or Oldenburg's *Soft Toilet* Ridler is playing with his art. This comic reaction directly connects with the viewer. The building creates a dialogue between the human and the art, and between art and life.

Little Big House is not an anomaly but is a cultural marker. It is evidence of a time, evidence of a belief in the role of art and the realization of a desire to fulfill seemingly impossible dreams. From modernism to the cultural transformation of the 1960s and 1970s, Little Big House is an art historical document. It is the full realization of a lifetime of training and experience within the most avant-garde and modernist circles, and transformed into a home. A home where a family, my family, has grown.

Morgan Ridler
Art History PhD candidate
The Gradate Center, CUNY
New York, NY

An Artist and Art Historian (Father/Daughter) Discussion on Zen, Materials, and Humor

Glenn Ridler and Morgan Ridler
May 11, 2017

Morgan: How do you define Zen? What does that mean to you?

Glenn: It means living in the moment. It means not hanging on to things either material or immaterial, like things you want to achieve, an agenda, a way of seeing life playing out and accepting it the way it comes, an appreciation of the common place, the everyday. I don't do this, but for real Zen people, this means right down to the breath you take each day. For me it means acceptance of the common place. To me it was the heart of Pop art. I didn't see the satirical or ironic qualities, even though one could see that, it wasn't what it was to me. It was celebration of the common.

M: The connection between art and life and art in the everyday is really connected to the Little Big House. Do you see that coming from other sources beside Zen?

G: I didn't really think about it as Zen at the time. I thought about it more as an evolution of modern art. Nobody was calling it Zen at the time. But looking back at it, that's what it was. I should have been aware of it. Dr. Suzuki and John Cage at the time were practicing Zen. And we never called it Zen. I don't think that makes any difference. Now that I think about it, it makes more sense to talk about it as Zen. It all happened with my teacher Paul Harris. He conducted the class in an almost Zen like way. I will never forget the first time we had to draw, he was talking about Hans Hofmann and push and pull. And I had no idea what he was talking about. So, when it came to drawing I just drew. He walked around and looked at everybody's work and he just said "No" and he walked on. And I was like huh. I expected an explanation of why "No." But he wanted me to find out why no. He had this philosophical way of talking that fascinated me. I did what I was supposed to do. I did all the work. The looking at it. The thinking about it. He got his doctorate at New School and Suzuki was teaching there or Columbia at the time. So, he was influenced for sure. Harris knew Cage as well, and he arranged for Cage to perform at Montclair. But Cage was asked to leave by the head of the music department, embarrassing Harris.

M: How to you think the Zen ideas or this process relates to how you work? Do you still work in that way?

G: These elements of Zen thinking still remain, yes. First of all a lot of my stuff doesn't have to be in a museum to be appreciated. They are outside of that genre.

M: Outside of high art?

G: Yeah. I am thinking of the DaMuse figures. The way they interact with life and mimic it and point out things about it by their actions.

M: What about how you work with materials? Is that Zen?

G: I never really thought about it that much but it is. For some artists, mastery of materials is the whole thing. When I went to school they didn't want you to be a sculptor and painter. You had to be a painter or a sculptor. That was it. I had to work my butt off to get a sculpture course. They wouldn't let me sign up. So eventually I talked the head of the department into letting me take it. I ended being a TA for that class. The approach to materials also occurred on the graduate level. We had a course "Design in Materials." The guy who was teaching was a Yale graduate. He had had Albers. And Albers's approach to materials was very experimental, trying things. I was never attached to one material. I enjoyed exploring the materials that lead to the purpose I was working on. The wire especially is an example of how I could take my two-dimensional drawing ability and apply it to the three-dimensional world. So some of my sculptures are three-dimensional drawings. It was an exploration of materials. It happened over a long period of time. But with other materials, wood is wood. It's a whole set of different parameters that fit some projects and not others. So I would explore mediums that way. With an openness to it. Applying it to a particular concept. That's why I think of myself as a conceptual artist. There is always an idea behind it. And then I find the material that suits that. A learning process with the material, not just single out and know one material. Not that one material, but many materials.

M: It seems like a lot of it was Bauhaus derived, from the foundations course and its exploration of materials. It's all connected. They didn't call it Zen there either. There was a great interest in non-western thought. Particularly Johannes Itten who started the foundations course and Albers later took over. Itten was interested in new wave religions. Not necessary Zen but eastern ideas. I think those things merge for you.

G: My therapist started me thinking about Zen again. I have the tendency to hold onto things I shouldn't. Regrets. I do a lot of anticipating. Anticipation is just something waiting for depression to happen. When you have a lot of expectations. And live your life that way. So I try to let go of some things.
We were talking about Zen I said, there would be no civilization if Zen was in control. We would have not technology. He said we wouldn't need it. In a Zen society everybody would be living pastoral life. It couldn't support a modern life. I said to myself I wondered Zen artist makes. So I looked it up and the definition was me. Its what I do. So I went back and thought about all the things in myself. Sure enough they were Zen, I just never called it that.

M: Have you ever thought about practicing Zen Buddhism? Mediation?

G: I have. When I came back from California I tried it fir a while. I did the candle mediation. I did that for a year. I ate organic diet. In 1968 there was nothing organic unless you grew it yours. We had a big garden.

M: Do you thing your most recent works relate to your interest in materials or Zen ideas?

G: You could make a case for the Zen interest in the common place. These creatures I have been making for the next show, *Aluminus Centipedus*, they're bugs. An abstraction of bug, somewhere between caterpillar and centipede. It's also a hold over from the common place.

Also the material. The big break through with this material was learning I could shoot a galvanized nail through the wire. It started with making cactus. I was trying all these different things with needle like objects. I tried drilling through the wire. It was very hard to do. I brook three or four bits in first 15 minutes. Your mother suggested the nail gun. Somehow I thought that possibility could work. Immediately I tried it and it worked. It was the play of tool with the material that enabled me to make the cactus and then the legs on the centipedes. A merger of tool and material. Any material has tools that go with it. The nail gun was a cross over. Nobody put nails through wire, they use wood. But I saw that it could switch over. I don't know how your mother thought of it, or what she was thinking.

M: What about coloring them?

G: Yes, that's new. For some reason I resisted that, because of my minimalist tendencies. I though the paint was extraneous for a long. For some reason I had an epiphany that they could easily be colored. That became a preoccupation with me. And I discovered another material, again, Day-Glo paint and I could give them a second life. When the lights went off they rise from the dead. And I was compulsed to do that. So have a whole bunch of creatures colored now.

M: Lets shift gears and discuss the house. Why do you think you are so fascinated by the illusion of the house? The little bigness. They way it fools the eye.

G: I really enjoyed optical illusions. When Op Art appeared I found it fascinating. I also found it devoid of emotion. I have always tried to bring those things together, ideas from the art world but also humanity. When I was working very abstract there was almost always a reconcilable subject. My severe, minimalist landscapes are like that. The illusion in the house was an attempt to give it a sense of play. When you looked at the house from a distance it appeared small, but extremely archetypal. The way a child would draw a house. A cultural meme. If you ask any kid to draw a house it would be similar to my house. I wanted when you walked up to it you became little. That was the play aspect to it. The fun aspect to it. A lot of my work has a sense of humor about it. The bugs I think are funny. Humorous. It's like that through all my stuff, in DaMuse, in the landscape paintings. It's in almost everything I ever made. There is a sense of humor about it. And that illusion allows you to play. The archetype. I was extremely fascinated in Carl Gustav Jung and his idea of the archetype. And also Plato with his cave and walls with prototype chair. So some of my chair stuff is from that. You can't ever see the archetype. You have to make it in your mind.

M: Anything else you want to discuss?

G: You know despite the fact that the house was meant to be a humorous kind of think. That your drive by and smile at. And if you were really interested get out and look at it and walk up and experience. You know, art as experience from John Dewey's book. That was in my head at the time too. Making art an experience. Not just something you look at but experience.

But the thing that has won out over time with the house is none of those things. It was the engineering aspect. How I made the house. Variation on a post and beam. That barn on the top of hill, a magnificent post and beam structure. I wondered my god how did they do this?

I like that look of the structure showing. I know I couldn't do that. I didn't have time for that, I was teaching full time. That's when I came up with the lamination idea and the look of post and beam without massive beams. I know I was going to be doing it by myself. Looking back it seems that all my works have some aspect of that.

The engineering aspect, solving a problem, nailing through the wire. When I made the new stuff the tools were worn out, I needed new tools. That was an engineering aspect. Making the nanotubes upside down. That was an engineering aspect too.

The playfulness too. I said this to myself the other day. "The serious Glenn makes the funny Glenn funny." Figuring out the engineering, how to make this thing, as opposed to the end product, which is supposed to be light and fun.

M: This has been great. Thanks,

G: Thanks.

Transcribed and Edited by Morgan Ridler, Ph.D.

Illustrations

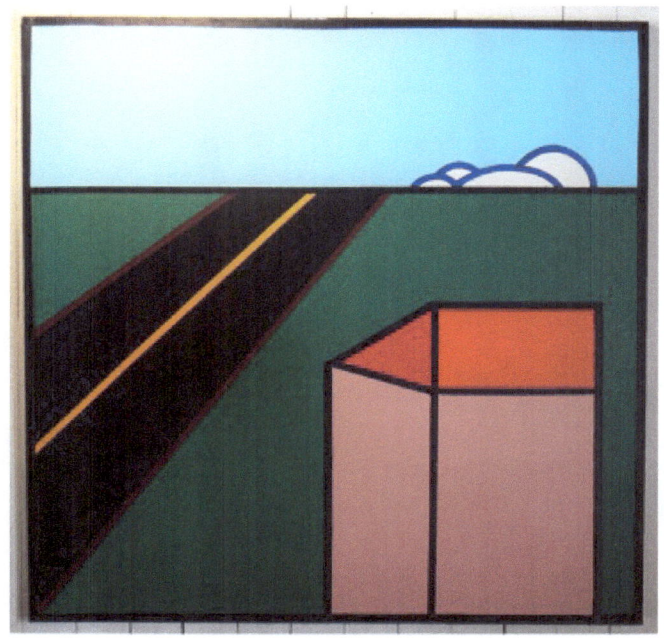

Figure 2: Glenn Ridler, *Minimalist Landscape*, 1967

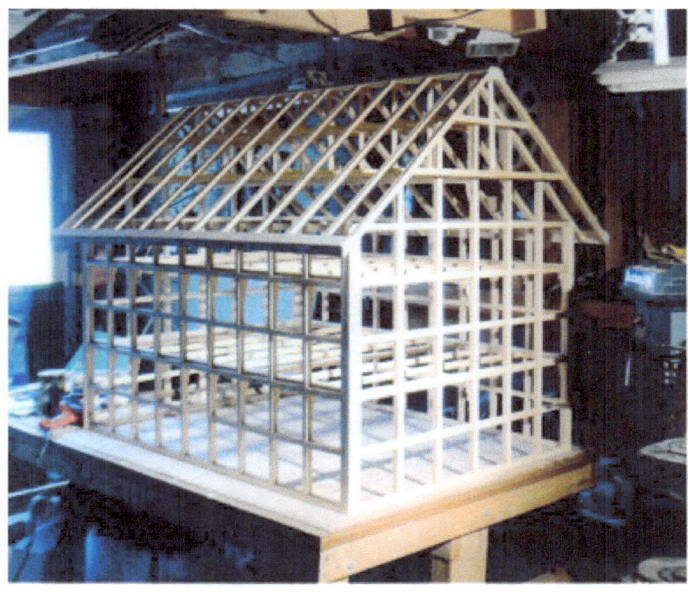

Figure 3: Glenn Ridler, *House Model*, 2008 Reconstruction of 1970 Original

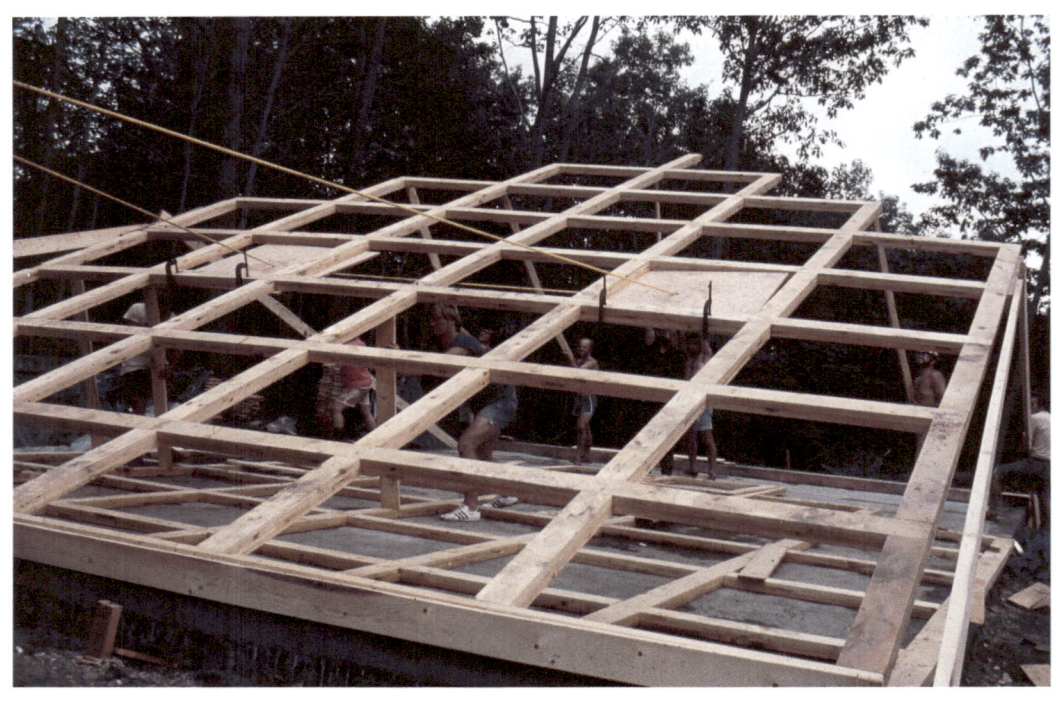

Figure 4: *Erection 2*, 1972

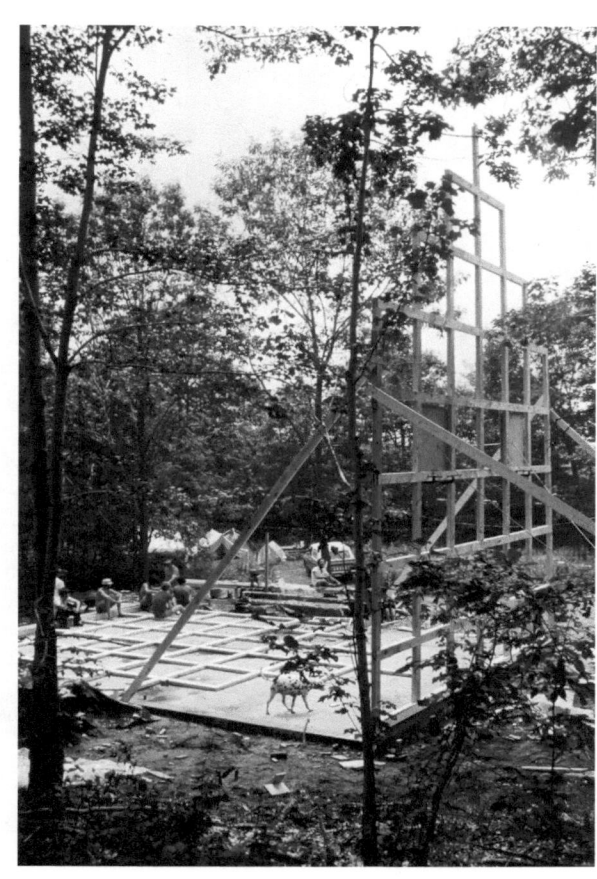

Figure 5: *One Wall Up*, 1972

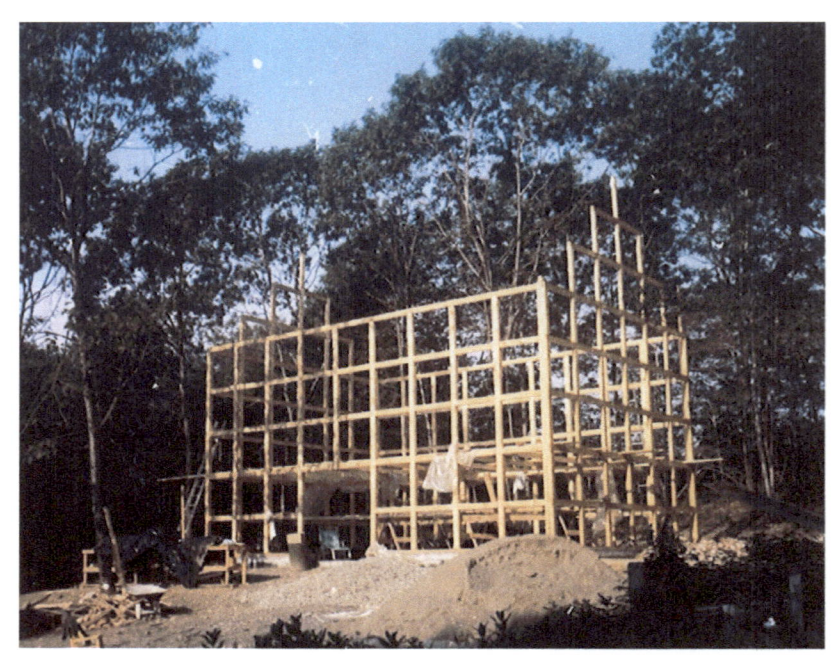

Figure 6: *Four Walls*, 1972

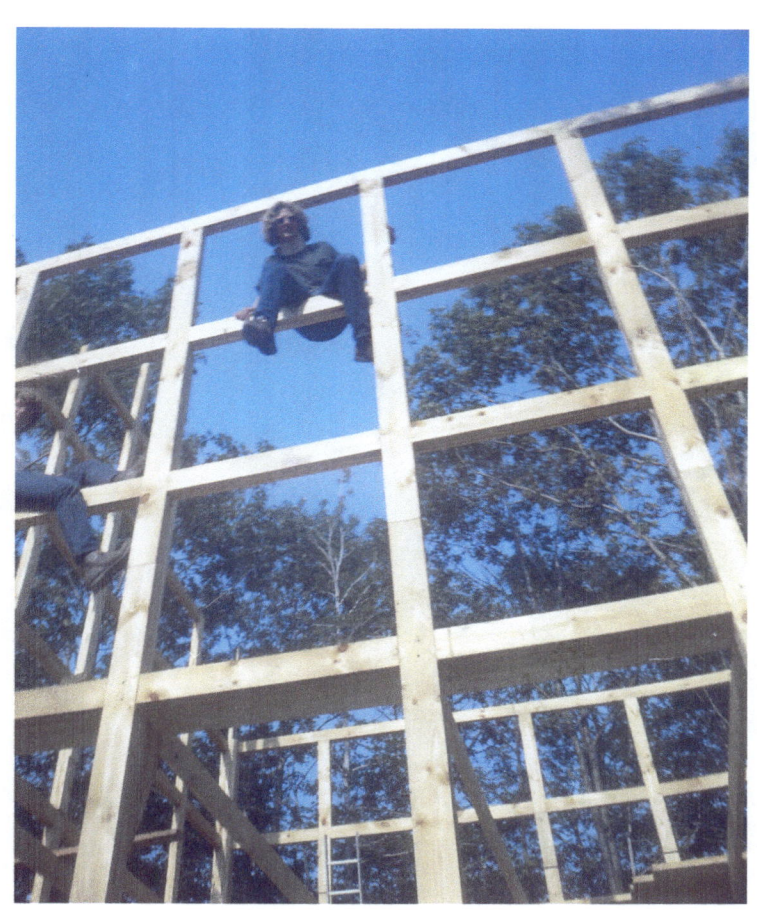

Figure 7: *Framed*, 1972

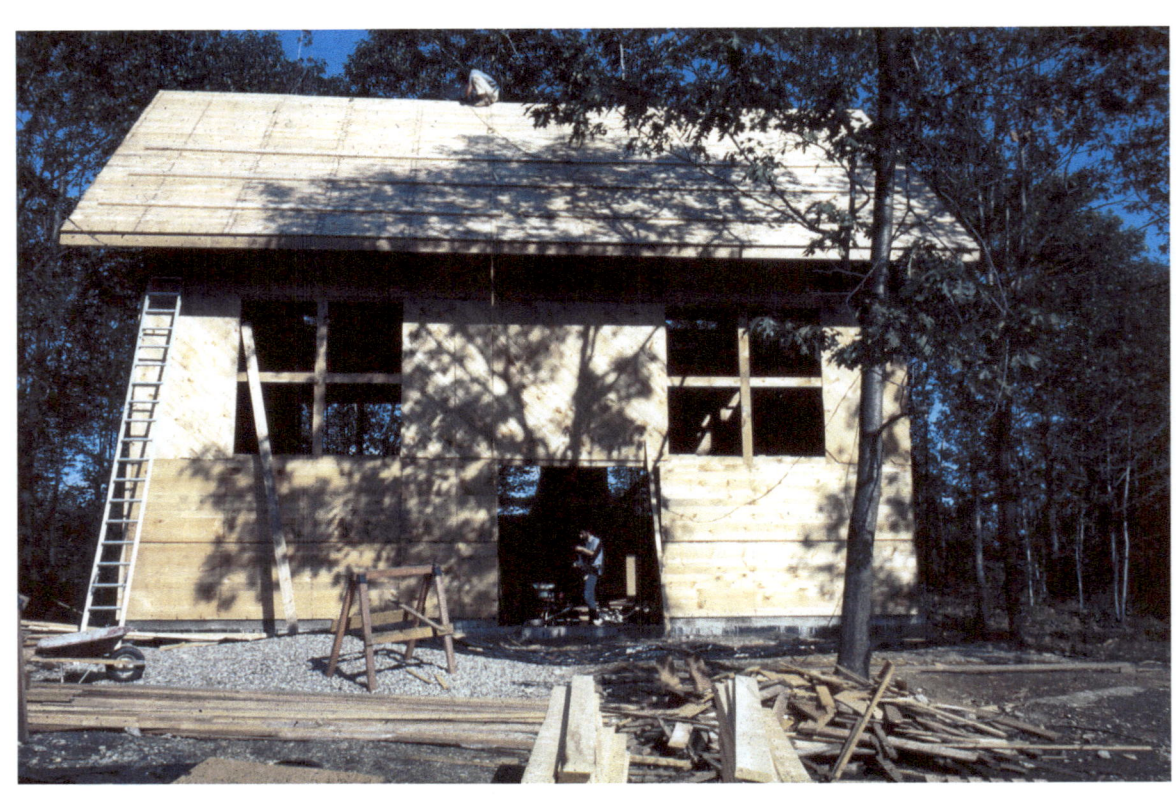

Figure 8: *Plywood*, 1972

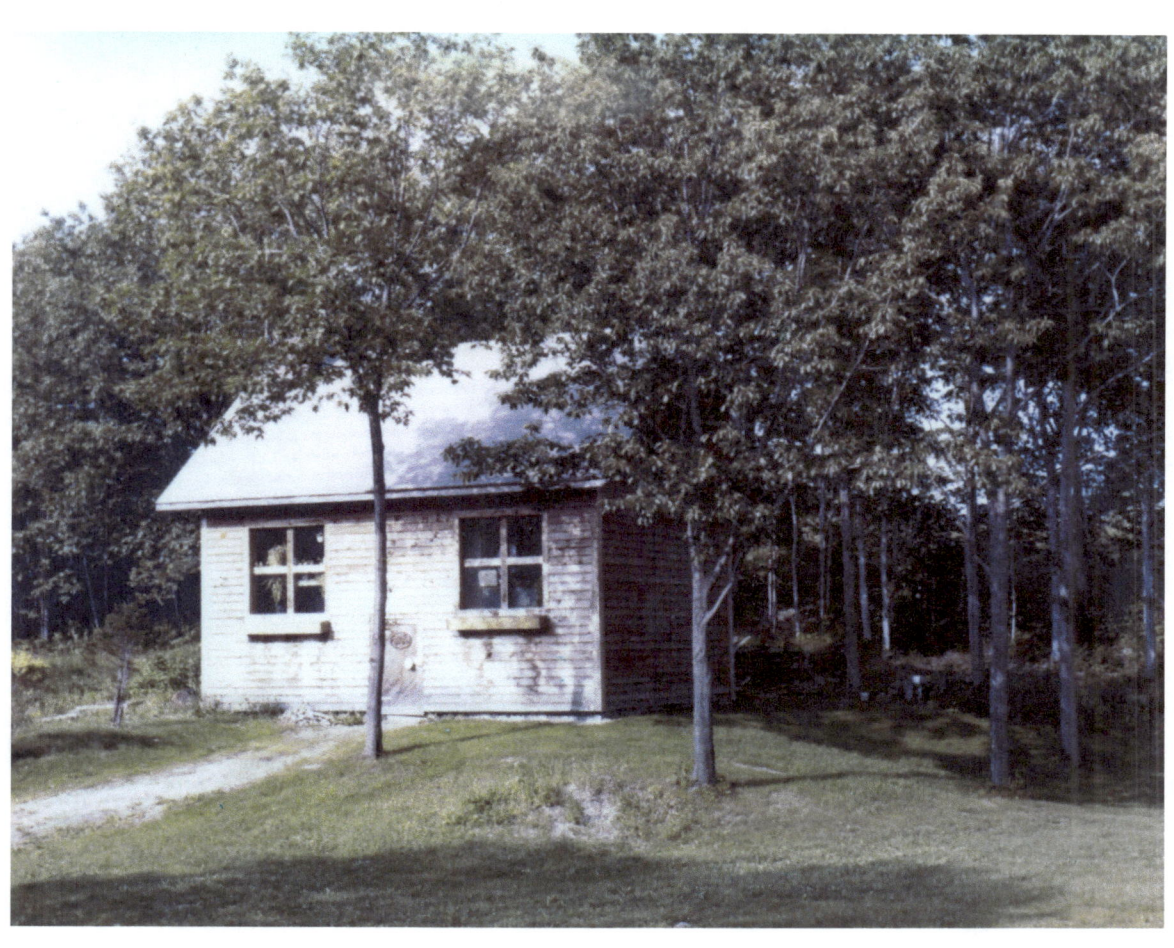

Figure 9: *No Gardens,* c. 1976

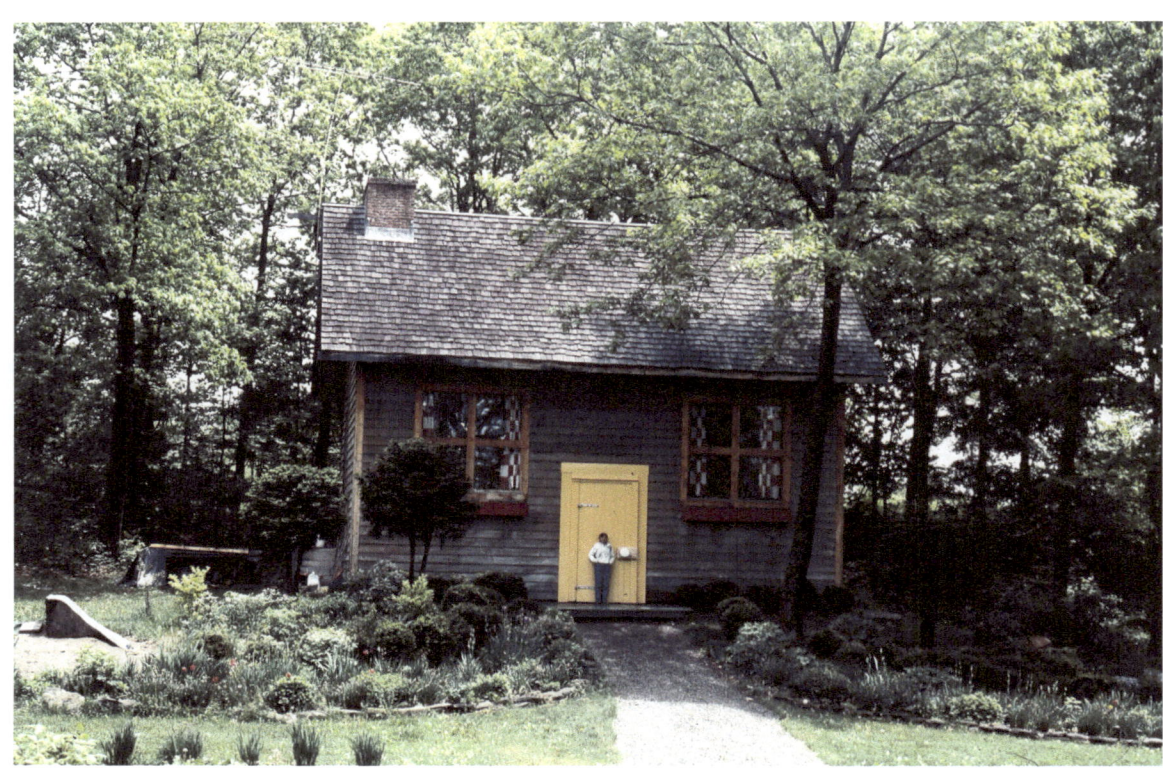

Figure 10: *Immature Garden*, c. 1985

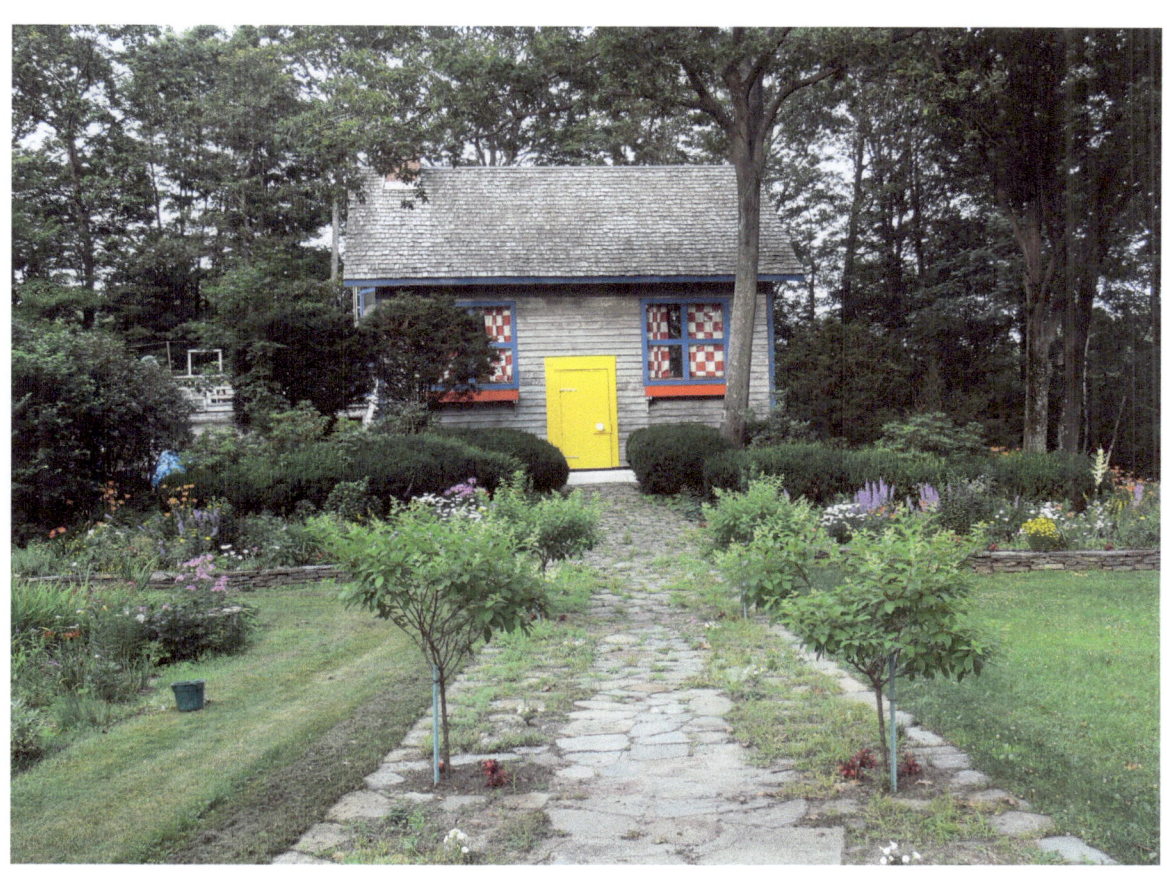

Figure 11: *Finished*, 2005

Little Big House Gallery Publication
2017

ISBN 978-0-692-83931-7